Tom Mitchell

FUN ❖ FAST ❖ EASY
DOG TRAINING
FOR KIDS

MITCHELL
MEDIA

Copyright © 2024 Mitchell Media, LLC. All Rights Reserved

No part of this book or any images herein may be reproduced in any form without permission in writing from the author. Reviewers may quote brief passages in reviews. While all attempts have been made to verify the information provided in this publication, neither the author nor the publisher assumes any responsibility for errors, omissions, or contrary interpretations of the subject matter herein. The views expressed in this publication are those of the author alone and should not be taken as expert instruction or commands. The reader is responsible for his or her own actions, as well as his or her own interpretation of the material found within this publication. Adherence to all applicable laws and regulations, including international, federal, state and local governing professional licensing, business practices, advertising, and all other aspects of doing business in the US, Canada or any other jurisdiction is the sole responsibility of the reader and consumer. Neither the author nor the publisher assumes any responsibility or liability whatsoever on behalf of the consumer or reader of this material. Any perceived slight of any individual or organization is purely unintentional.

Illustrations by Emanuel Pretonari

Cover design by Kes Lehrman & Olivia Hinchley

Paperback ISBN: 978-1-7331645-5-9

Ebook ISBN-978-1-7331645-4-2

First Mitchell Media LLC edition • February 2024

Acknowledgments

I am deeply grateful to my remarkable team for their support throughout the creation of this book. For years, I have dreamed of enhancing people's relationships with their dogs. It is with heartfelt appreciation that I acknowledge the contributions of everyone who helped this dream become a reality.

Special gratitude is extended to Kes Lehrman and Olivia Hinchley, whose creativity and collaboration helped bring this project to life. Your encouragement, insight, and aloha spirit infused every step of this journey. Thank you.

To Emanuel Pretonari, thank you for your extraordinary illustrations, which breathe life into the narrative. Your talent and creativity have added a magical dimension to this book.

To Marcy Tippmann, thank you for your exceptional design talent. Your expertise and attention to detail brought this book to its fullest potential.

To all those whose support and expertise have contributed to this project, thank you for sharing my passion for improving the bond between humans and their dogs. Your contributions have made a lasting impact. I am truly grateful for the privilege of collaborating with such a talented and dedicated team.

With deepest appreciation,

Tom Mitchell

Dedication

To my two daughters, Malia and Kiana.

Your love of animals continues to inspire me.

To Samara; thank you for your love and support.

And to Linda Tellington-Jones, founder of the Tellington TTouch, her sister Robyn Hood, and all the TTouch practitioners worldwide for bringing awareness and kindness to the world of animal training.

And last, to Michelle and Kea, you live in my Heart and Soul.

Testimonials

"When I first met Tom Mitchell in the early 1980s, I did not imagine he would become a lifelong friend, advisor, and someone responsible for helping to spread the Tellington method for companion animals across the globe. For over 30 years, Tom has focused on helping people develop a relationship with dogs by promoting an attitude of kindness and gratitude for our canine friends. He clearly demonstrates that the concept of having to be the "alpha dog" has been thoroughly discredited by the American Behavioral Veterinary Association. Many studies have proven the effectiveness of the simple one-and-a-quarter TTouch circles for reducing fear and pain and enhancing a state of well-being."

- Linda Tellington-Jones, Founder of the TTouch®

"The 1 Minute Dog Training System really works! Our dog now comes with ease now because you taught us how to give him the right kind of positive reinforcement. It feels so much easier and more doable in 1 Minute segments."

- Char, Dr. William Showalter and Scooby

"I had the most positive experience with the 1 Minute Dog Training! When I took my dog Buffalo to the local dog training class, they were too rigid and strict. Our work with the 1 Minute Dog Technique was perfect for both our temperaments… gentle and joyful, but firm. I highly recommend the 1 Minute Dog Training and TTouch work. There is a deep respect and care for animals and a positive life attitude that is a nourishing and instructive combination."

– Linda Reuther and Buffalo

"When my dog Mico was young and I took him for a walk, he would pull me down the street. If he saw another dog, he pulled even harder. After a few short sessions, I was amazed that Mico listened and did not pull anymore. On top of that, he has matured into an awesome dog and this training played a great role in that. I highly recommend 1 Minute Dog Training! This is the best training method in the world!"

- Basha Cohen and Mico

Disclaimer (Please Read)

Tom Mitchell, 1 Minute Dog Training, One Minute Dog LLC, and Mitchell Media, LLC cannot be held responsible for any injury or damage resulting from dog training activities. If you are unsure about any aspect of dog training, please consult a professional in your area, or your veterinarian. This book describes a proven training method for dog training. It does not cure dogs with aggression problems, or predatory aggression. Please ensure you take all reasonable precautions to prevent injury to others (including dogs). While all attempts have been made to verify information provided in this publication, the Publisher assumes no responsibility for errors, omissions, or contrary interpretation of the subject matter herein. Any perceived slights of specific persons, peoples, or organizations are unintentional. In practical advice books, like anything else in life, there are no guarantees! Readers are cautioned to rely on their own judgment, and those of outside professionals about their individual circumstances and their dog and act accordingly.

About the Author

THAT'S ME! WHEN I WAS 2 YEARS OLD

Hi, I'm Tom Mitchell.

I wrote this book with lots of help from my dog Roxy.

Most people know me as the 1 Minute Dog Trainer. I've been working with dogs since I was a kid just like you!"

This is a picture of me with my very first dog. Her name was Sandy. We were BEST friends.

She showed me how much it's possible to love our dogs.

"I love all animals. And I've spent my whole life working with them. I've worked with horses, cats, wolves, and even rhinos too! I've had so much fun and learned a lot.

Now, I've been a dog trainer for over 30 years. That's a LONG time! I'm so excited to show you how to train your dog. Let's do it!

Table of Contents

Chapter One 14
Awesome Adventures with Roxy!

Chapter Two 24
The Best of Friends

Chapter Three 28
Training 1 Minute at a Time

Chapter Four 32
Speaking to Your Dog

Chapter Five 38
The 3 Most Important Training Steps

Chapter Six 48
Treat Time with Your Pup

Chapter Seven 56
The Language of Love

Chapter Eight 62
Even Superheroes Feel Afraid Sometimes

Chapter Nine 68
Unconditional Love

Chapter Ten 74
Walking Your Dog

Chapter Eleven 82
The Scoop on Picking Up Poop

Chapter Twelve 90
    Meeting Other Dogs

Chapter Thirteen 100
    Dogs in the Morning and at Night

Chapter Fourteen 106
    Puppies and Grown-Up Dogs

Chapter Fifteen 112
    How to Show Your Dog Love with **TTouches**

Chapter Sixteen 116
    How I Learned Potty Training

Chapter Seventeen 122
    Happy Hellos and Jumping Pups

Chapter Eighteen 126
    Your Family is Not a Wolf Pack

Chapter Nineteen 132
    Woof!

Chapter Twenty 140
    Bath Time Fun

Final Thoughts 144

to Get the FREE Guides

LIFETIME GUARANTEE

We're committed to your satisfaction! If you ever feel unsatisfied with your purchase, please reach out to us at **info@1minutedog.com** for a prompt and full refund.

Foreword

Hey there! Before you jump into this super cool book full of fun stories, awesome pictures, and tips on training your dog, guess what? I've got some extra special stuff for you!

I have all these neat videos and guides that you can watch for FREE, and they're all about how to train your puppy.

It's like having a puppy coach right in your home!

To get these awesome freebies, all you need to do is go to www.1minutedog.com. If you are 13 or older, you'll type in your email. If you are younger than 13, please ask your parents to sign up. You can see so many cool things: Tips on how to take care of your dog every day, how to keep him healthy and happy, and even updates on doggy food. Plus, you'll get to see my special surprises!

I hope you have a blast with all these videos and guides I made just for you.

Happy reading and happy dog training!

CHAPTER 1

Awesome Adventures with Roxy!

HI THERE! I'M ROXY. I'll be your expert guide to the amazing world of dogs. I'm here to show you how to make training your dog fun and easy.

I'm so excited you're here! Together, we are going to learn all about dogs.

As a dog myself, I'll be really great at helping you understand your dog. I have TONS of experience with this stuff.

Do you have a dog? If not, I hope you get one soon. If so, you're lucky to have a dog in your life!

And your dog will be so lucky to have you.

I love my family more than anything in the world. I've been with them since I was 12 weeks old. They have helped me learn and grow in the same way that I am going to help you learn.

I live with two grown-ups and two kids. I love each person in my family, no matter what!

I love my family because they showed me that I can trust them. Trust is very important for us dogs. It helps us feel safe.

Each dog is special. Each person is special. And together, your relationship is one-of-a-kind.

I'm a Belgian Malinois, and my breed is known for being smart and hardworking.

In fact, my pals even have jobs protecting the White House and keeping the President safe. That's a big deal!

That's right—dogs can have jobs too. There are therapy dogs, seeing eye dogs, police dogs, search and rescue dogs, lifeguard dogs, military dogs, dogs who protect people, and more. We help humans every day!

Did you know there are over 400 breeds of dogs? That's a lot of variety.

Dogs are different just like you're different from your classmates, your friends, and maybe even your brother or sister.

Each dog breed has its own personality. They come in all shapes, colors, and sizes too.

Think of a Chihuahua and a Great Dane. When you look at these two breeds, you can see how different they are.

Breeds look different and act in unique ways too.

Take my friend Toby, for example.

He's a lapdog, meaning he loves to cuddle with his family all day.

Lapdogs are usually small and cuddly, but sometimes big dogs think they're lapdogs too—oops!

Then there's my buddy, Sophie. She's a Labrador Retriever (codename: Lab).

Labs are famous for being "seeing eye dogs." Sophie helps blind people stay safe.

She's really smart and helps people cross the street when they can't see cars.

Labs are also amazing family pets. Do you know any Labs?

Okay, so there are lots of breeds and different jobs that dogs do. But what is something we all have in common?

Well, all dogs have SUPERPOWERS!

Yup, you read that right.

Some dogs use their powers to be heroes.

Lucy, my super-sniffer Bloodhound friend helps find lost people or bad guys.

Others, like your dog, might use their powers to be your best friend. That's an important job, too.

But here's the secret: dogs need your help to unlock their superpowers. And you hold the magic key. That key is dog training!

In this book, we'll explore the wonderful world of dogs, from their noses to their toes.

I'll share with you how to love and train your dog.

I want to help you become best friends.

So, grab a treat and follow me, and let's get started on this paw-some adventure together!

CHAPTER 2

The Best of Friends

DID YOU KNOW THAT dogs and people have been best friends for a loooong time?

It's true! Dogs really are humans best friends. We have a special connection that goes back thousands and thousands of years.

Our history together is amazing. Did you know that dogs used to be wolves? Yep! A super long time ago, humans and wolves worked together.

Wolves helped people hunt, and people shared their food with them.

We're going to talk more about wolves later on. Why? Because there is so much more to learn about dogs and wolves. Today, even though we are cousins, we're really not the same.

We dogs have become your guardians, soul mates, and play pals—all rolled into one!

So how do we make this dog-human relationship work? Simple. By learning from each other every day.

Think about puppies. They've got a lot to learn—from not chewing on your favorite shoes to understanding where to go potty.

But guess what? You have a lot to learn too! And that's where I come in to help.

Dogs don't always think like humans. We might want to, but we're pretty different—just look at us!

My goal here is to help you think like a dog. I'll also show you how to help your dog understand you.

Remember that learning takes time. But do you know what speeds up learning? It's doing something over and over again. This is how you strengthen your dog's superpowers.

And guess what? I'm going to show you the fastest way to learn, 1 minute at a time. My family trained me this way and I learned very quickly! My family trained many other dogs, too. We're all great friends now.

So, as we emBARK on this journey together, let me show you how you and your dog can learn more every day.

Let's Review

- 🐾 Dogs and humans have been best friends for a really long time.

- 🐾 Pups and people teach each other some of the most important lessons in life.

- 🐾 Dogs can learn to listen really well where there's love and understanding.

CHAPTER 3

Training 1 Minute at a Time

THINK OF ALL THE things you can do in about a minute.

You can make your bed, take out the trash, floss your teeth, put your dirty clothes in the hamper, drink a glass of water, or practice your dog training skills!

These tasks only take 1 minute, but they make a big difference. And training your dog a few times a day for only a minute can also make a big difference.

So, making your bed and taking out the trash helps the adults in your life. And drinking water and flossing your teeth helps you stay healthy.

And training your dog regularly is the best way to have a great friendship!

Most days, you drink more than one glass of water or brush your teeth at least a couple of times, right? I hope so!

Well, you can practice dog training more than once a day too. It doesn't take much time. In fact, it only takes 1 minute! And I'm going to show you how.

REMEMBER:

You can make your dog's superpowers even stronger with training. Pick two or three 1-minute blocks to work on training. YES! 1 minute of training a couple of times a day makes a difference. Training leads to a closer friendship with your dog.

Let's Review

- Dog training doesn't have to be a long process.

- You can train your pup 1 minute at a time and still get excellent results.

- The more you train your dog, the greater her powers will be—and the better your friendship will become!

CHAPTER 4

Speaking to Your Dog

BEFORE WE TALK ABOUT training your dog, let's talk about how to speak to your dog.

When we are born, most dogs cannot understand human language. That would be an EXTRA-SUPERDOG!

Even human babies don't understand human language. But we dogs are smart enough to learn human words really fast.

It's another one of our superpowers. Some dogs know more words than other dogs. And dogs around the world understand different languages.

Dogs learn whichever language our families speak. Most dogs can learn 100-200 words. Some dogs can even learn 1000 words! Amazing, right?

And just like people, dogs learn language by listening to your words and how you act. We look for clues all around us.

It helps to know that your dog LOVES routine. For example, if you always ask him to "please sit" before you give him his meal, he will most likely sit faster than at other times.

And now it is time to think like a dog. We like making you happy!

Your words, tone of voice, and body language let us know if we're doing a good job. It's truly all we want!

How am I supposed to listen to you when we don't speak the same language!?

Think of how excited we get when you tell us "Good dog!"

Many dog trainers tell people that they should only speak to their dogs one word at a time. They say you should only say "sit" as a command.

Do you like being commanded? Or do you like being asked politely?

Imagine if your teacher told you what to do or commanded you... One. Word. At. A. Time. If that happened, you probably wouldn't be able to read this book! It would take too long to learn the language.

You know so many words because people use them when talking to you.

I'm guessing your teacher doesn't just point at you and say, "Read." They probably ask, "Will you please sit quietly and read?"

It's a nicer way of asking and probably makes you feel happier about reading.

This may be different than what you've heard before, but we dogs like it when you speak to us in complete sentences.

We might not understand everything you say at first, but we like to hear your voice—especially if it's kind! We are your best friends, after all.

Remember, your tone of voice and body language matter.

Dogs like it when you ask us nicely, too. Instead of pointing at your dog and yelling, "Sit," you could ask, "Would you please sit?"

Hand signals can help your dog learn words. Make sure your hand signals are soft rather than harsh.

When you ask your dog to stay, you could use a soft hand as a signal for "stay."

You can see this in the image above.

You can pick the hand signals you like best. Just make sure each signal is clear and different.

Dogs are really smart, but we need you to be clear when asking us to do something!

Let's Review

🐾 Your dog likes hearing your kind voice.

🐾 We learn language through a mixture of words, signals, routine, and other clues.

🐾 Talk to us in complete sentences to help us learn.

🐾 Hand signals help us as long as you use different signals for different requests.

CHAPTER 5
The 3 Most Important Training Steps

IT'S TIME TO TALK about the three most important steps when training your puppy. Remember, while dogs' superpower is learning, yours is teaching.

Think about how you learned to read. First, you had to learn the alphabet. Then, you learned how to put those letters together to make words.

Finally, you learned how to group enough words together to create a sentence.

And now here you are, reading this B-O-O-K!

Your dog will learn how to use his superpowers just like you learned how to read. But instead of teaching your dog the ABCs, teach him SSC:

- **Sit** - **Stay** - **Come**

Once your dog can sit, stay, and come, he'll be ready to learn so much more. Just like you can read this sentence because you know your ABCs.

Each new skill you teach your dog will start with sit, stay, and come.

In the beginning, it may be good to have a grown-up with you. They can help when you first practice these skills with your dog.

Let's start with SIT:

When I first learned how to sit, my family had to help me into the right position. Be careful though, and make sure you're gentle when showing your dog how to sit.

You might hurt your dog if you push on him too hard. Ouch!

Instead, think about the way your knees bend. Well, your dog's knees bend the same way too. Has someone ever pressed behind your knees before? It probably made your knees bend, right?

You can do this to show your dog how to sit, too. Just remember to be very gentle!

Here's how to teach SIT:

1. Place one arm across the back of your dog's hind legs.

2. Gently press behind your dog's knees. This should ease him into a "sit."

3. As soon as your dog's bottom touches the ground, say, "Sit, please!"

4. Give him a treat and tell him he's a good dog. This is the best part!

STAY and COME:

Once your dog sits, you can teach him how to stay and come.

You might need a helper to show your dog what you mean when you say "stay."

1. After your dog sits, hold out your hand and back away slowly. Ask your dog, "Will you stay, please?" It may help to have someone hold your dog still while you practice this.

2. Once you've backed away a few feet, call your dog to come to you. Say, "Come here, good boy!" You can also use your dog's name—I always know to come running whenever I hear "Roxy!"

3. Your dog should come straight to you. As soon as he does, ask him to sit again.

4. Give him a treat, love, and some kisses.

5. Act super excited EVERY time your dog comes when you call.

It's important to never call your dog to punish him.

If my family called out to me and I came running just to be yelled at, I probably wouldn't want to come next time! Thankfully, they've never done that.

YOU WANT YOUR DOG TO KNOW THAT THERE'S A PARTY WAITING EVERY TIME SHE HEARS HER NAME CALLED.

The skill "come" is the most important one for us to know.

Dogs don't always know if a car is coming or if there's something dangerous around the corner. But we can understand that being called means we drop everything else and run to you!

Every day you want to practice this important skill two or three times, just for 1 minute at a time. These skills are the most important for us to know. And you can teach your dog that this is fun and exciting!

> My favorite is practicing sit, stay, and come with a ball. Here's how it usually goes:
>
> 1. My family will ask me to sit.
> 2. Then, they tell me to stay while they throw the ball.
> 3. When it's high in the air, they tell me to go get it.
> 4. I use my superpowers to run and catch the ball. Then my family calls me to come back, and I come running every time.
> 5. I sit down one more time and drop the ball.

My family is always so proud of my catch. They tell me what a good girl I am, and we do the whole thing again.

Please be careful with older dogs that may get tired or sore easily.

THE MORE YOU PRACTICE, THE MORE SKILLED YOUR PUP WILL BECOME.

Remember, your dog has superpowers that become stronger and stronger with daily training!

I like to practice all day long. Think about what works best for you. Is it easier to practice in the morning or at night? I like both!

You can have a 1 minute training session in the morning and another when you come home from school. If you plan it out in your mind, it will be more likely to happen.

Share your plan with your dog too! Let her know when you want to practice together. Think of it like making plans with your friends. It gives you both something to look forward to.

Let's Review

- Sit, stay, and come are the three most important skills you can teach your dog.

- It may take us a bunch of tries to learn, so keep practicing every day even just for 1 minute at a time.

- An adult can help you practice these skills.

- Praise your dog every time he comes when called.

CHAPTER 6
Treat Time with Your Pup

HAVE YOUR PARENTS EVER asked you to empty the dishwasher, put your clean clothes away, or do your homework? Did they motivate you with an allowance, a fun activity, dessert, or a toy you really wanted?

It probably worked, right? Well, dogs don't get an allowance because we don't care about money. But a nice treat, an exciting toy, or a great belly rub? Now we're talking.

When you give your puppy a treat for doing something good, he will keep doing it. Just like how you do chores and maybe even your homework for a reward.

Your dog will also love playing with you as a reward for his hard work.

If he does something you want him to keep doing, you can play a quick game together. Fetch, catch, tug-of-war, a treasure hunt— you name it!

We love all rewards, but we reallyyyy love food. We love it so much that we might even try to eat it out of the trash!

I always want to try my family's food. I look at them with my best, biggest puppy-dog eyes. Sometimes it works, and sometimes it doesn't.

Most families don't want to feed their dog at the table. That's probably a good idea.

Some human snacks are okay to share with your pup. Just make sure you check with your parents or your vet first!

> Some human foods are **mega dangerous** for dogs. It's very important to **NEVER** share these foods with your pup:
>
> - Chocolate
> - Grapes
> - Raisins
> - Corn on the cob (corn off the cob is OK)
> - Onions
> - Garlic
> - Xylitol (a sugar-free sweetener found in stuff like gum, candy, and toothpaste)
> - Macadamia nuts

My advice? Always ask an adult before giving your pup human food.

One time, my buddy Oscar ate a whole bag of chocolate chips. He got really sick and had to go to the hospital.

It was the middle of the night, and his family was so scared.

Thankfully, Oscar's veterinarian worked quickly and they saved his life. But it was a close call!

His family was very careful sharing human food after that.

Some fruits and veggies are great to use for training but check with an adult to make sure it's okay. Just stay away from the chocolate chips!

Here's another important thing to know:

Dogs LOVE treats.

We love them so much we don't know when to stop eating them.

It's your job to give us the right amount of treats. We may always ask you for more, but it's unhealthy for us to eat too many.

Think about when your parents give you ice cream for doing chores. They won't let you eat the entire carton, right? If you've ever done that, you know it can hurt your tummy.

The same thing goes for your favorite candy. Too much of a yummy thing can make you sick—and no one wants to feel that way, ever.

Your dog is the same way. It's great to give her treats, but she can get sick if you give her too many. And when your dog gets sick, someone has to clean it up. YUCK! That someone might be you. And who wants that job?

Your pup might feel icky and *ruff* if she eats too many treats once in a while. But she could have an even bigger problem if you feed her too many treats all the time.

What kind of problem? Well, being overweight is not good for your dog. Chubby puppies are adorable, but it's important that your dog stays a healthy size.

You can help by feeding your dog a healthy amount of treats. You can also help by giving her lots of daily exercise. Exercise can be a blast. Walks, runs, playing catch—all of these activities make us so happy!

Let's talk about dog diets. There are a lot of different dog diets. I like to eat some raw meat and other delicious foods. Some people feed their dog dry kibble dog food. Some diets are healthier than others.

Veterinarians have learned that what you feed your dog is one of the more important ways to keep them healthy.

I want to give you some free goodies about treats, training, and keeping your puppy healthy. You can scan this code if you want to learn more with your family.

SCAN ME to Get the FREE Guides

Let's Review

- 🐾 Treats or pieces of kibble are a wonderful way to help train your dog.

- 🐾 Some human foods are okay for your pup but not all. Always ask an adult what foods to feed your dog.

- 🐾 Too many treats can hurt your puppy, so switch between treats, toys, play, and cuddles as rewards.

- 🐾 Help your dog stay at her healthiest weight by giving her daily exercise.

CHAPTER 7

The Language of Love

THINK ABOUT YOUR FAVORITE stuffed animal. How much do you love it? So much!

And how good does it feel to hug and squeeze it as tightly as you can? It's the best.

Well, you probably want to hug and squeeze your puppy because you love him so much!

But here's the thing: you want to make sure it feels good for your puppy, too.

Let's think like your dog for a moment. Would you want to be squeezed too tightly? Probably not.

So, let's see how you can show your puppy love in a way that makes him feel safe and happy.

I personally love it when my people rub their hands down my back with soft strokes. Gentle touches can show your puppy how much you love her.

Special touches on the back of my head feel wonderful. Letting your puppy decide when and how you cuddle will make her feel loved.

Just like humans, some dogs love snuggles, and some don't.

You're bigger than your puppy, so think of how you'd feel if you traded places.

Imagine if a big animal (maybe ten times bigger than you) ran up to you. Then, it opened its arms, and looked even bigger! It jumped on top of you and squeezed super hard.

EEK! That would feel really scary.

But I've got some good news. You can practice snuggling your puppy or even an older dog. Here are the important points:

Snuggling Softly

1. If your puppy or dog is new, walk up to her slowly.
2. Talk to her calmly.
3. Squat down. Give your dog a gentle touch to let her know you are there.
4. If your dog is happy, you can sit down next to her. Please make sure your dog feels safe and comfortable.

An adult should help you and watch closely, especially if you have a new dog or puppy.

If you have a small dog or a puppy, you may want to pick her up. But if you have a big dog, it might weigh more than you do! I don't recommend trying to pick up a big dog.

Again, make sure an adult is with you when you first try holding your puppy.

You want your dog to feel happy and not afraid of being held. If your puppy wiggles or squirms when you hold her, it's important to listen to what her body is saying.

Dogs talk with our bodies. It's one of our superpowers.

If your puppy wiggles, gently set her down following these steps:

1. Keep holding your puppy against your chest. Slowly bend your knees to get closer to the ground.

2. Once you're squatted down, you can move your puppy away from your chest.

3. Gently place your dog on the ground. Make sure her paws touch down safely before you let go of her body.

The more gentle and caring you are, the more your dog will know how much you love her.

What do your dog and your phone have in common?

They both have collar I.D.

Let's Review

🐾 Watch your puppy's body language to learn what she likes and doesn't like.

🐾 Always ask an adult for help when you hold your puppy.

🐾 Use a calm, quiet voice when you hold your puppy.

🐾 Keep your pup close to your body but don't squeeze her too tight. You want your puppy to trust that you've got her, but you don't want to squish her.

CHAPTER 8

Even Superheroes Feel Afraid Sometimes

DO YOU EVER FEEL afraid of ghosts, monsters, or something that isn't even real?

Many people feel much safer when they cuddle up with their dog. Being a good protector is one of our superpowers.

Even though dogs can be brave in times of trouble, we get scared too. And when we're afraid, we may need your help.

So, how can you help your pup feel safe? Well, this is another time when it helps to think like a dog.

Your pup probably isn't afraid of the monster from that scary book you read the other night. But imagine being a dog on New Year's Eve or the 4th of July.

Your dog doesn't understand that people like to celebrate some holidays with fireworks.

BOOM! POP! BOOM!

Suddenly, there are massive explosions in the sky right above your head. You would probably be terrified too if you didn't know what fireworks were!

Plus, super-strong hearing is another one of our superpowers. So, fireworks aren't just loud to us, they're REALLY LOUD!

Even though you know your dog is safe, he might not be so sure.

When your dog is scared, do your best to keep him calm. Speak in a soft voice. Gently pet your dog only where he likes to be touched.

Dogs usually feel safer under a bed or in a small closet when they're frightened. Help your dog find a safe space if this happens.

This is not a good time to let your dog outside alone. Some dogs can become so afraid they will escape your yard and run away.

This happened to my friend Duke one time. He was in the yard when a bunch of fireworks exploded right over his head.

He got so freaked out that he jumped right over the fence! He ran and ran to get away from the fireworks.

He ran so far away that he couldn't find his way back home. He was scared and just wanted to be with his family again.

Thankfully, Duke's family spent the whole night looking for him. They found him after hours of searching. They made sure to keep him inside anytime there were fireworks after that.

If your dog gets freaked out whenever there are loud noises, ask if your parents can get him a Thundershirt. A Thundershirt will feel like a gentle hug to your dog. This really helps me calm down.

Or I can show you how to make a Thundershirt at home if you want. What you need to do is get what's called an ACE bandage. You can ask your parents what this is.

I call this the Calming Wrap. You can wrap the bandage around your dog's body like in this picture.

This is really important:
Please make sure it is not too tight.

You want your dog to move around comfortably without feeling squeezed too tightly.

Whenever I wear my Calming Wrap, I feel much safer. I tell all my doggie friends to try it if they're scared of loud noises!

Other things might scare your dog too. This could be other animals, the doorbell ringing, a bath, getting her nails clipped, people wearing costumes, thunderstorms, and Halloween decorations, to name a few.

Different dogs may respond to fear in different ways. Some may run and hide, some may bark, and some might even become so afraid that they try to protect themselves by biting.

Now that you know some of the things to do when your dog is scared, you can help your dog overcome fears! Your love and friendship can help your pup feel safer.

Let's Review

- 🐾 Watch your dog for clues about how she is feeling.

- 🐾 You can comfort your dog with calm words and gentle touches when he is scared.

- 🐾 Thundershirts or a Calming Wrap can help dogs feel safer.

- 🐾 Small spaces may help a dog feel safer. Please keep your dog inside when she is afraid.

CHAPTER 9

Unconditional Love

HAVE YOU EVER HEARD of "unconditional love?" This means that you love someone or something no matter what.

Many people share unconditional love with their family. They might get upset and argue with these people, but they will always love them.

Many people will also say they have unconditional love for their dogs. Do you have unconditional love for your dog?

Your dog can teach you so much about love. He doesn't care if you failed that test, lost that game, or embarrassed yourself in front of your friends.

As long as you love your dog, he will love you no matter who you are. Unconditional love is another one of our superpowers.

I feel so lucky to have my family. As I said before, trust is very important for us dogs. It helps us feel safe.

So why do I trust my family? Because they are kind to me. It's that simple. They treat me with kindness and have always been gentle with me. My family and I have an amazing relationship. We all love each other no matter what.

But some dogs don't have as much trust with their family. Some people can be mean to their dogs.

Some dogs get choked a lot, shocked with electric collars, or even hit. This can make a dog mean, even if they don't want to be.

And then, their dogs can't trust them. They don't share unconditional love.

Do you know what a scientific study is? Maybe you have learned about these in school.

This is when scientists look at a lot of different people and their dogs and find out what happens to dogs when people do different things.

Some people hurt their dogs on purpose. The scientists have found out that when this happens, dogs can be mean to people, their families, and especially children.[1]

So, always be careful if you don't know a dog well. You never know if someone has been unkind to their dog. This might make the dog feel afraid. And fearful dogs are the most likely to act mean.

I don't know why someone would ever want to hurt a dog. As a dog myself, I can promise that your pup just wants to make you happy.

---

1 Siracusa, C. (2015). "A Punished Dog Is an Aggressive Dog." Psychology Today. Retrieved from https://www.psychologytoday.com/au/blog/canine-corner/201508/punished-dog-is-aggressive-dog

Sharing trust and kindness creates unconditional love. So how can you be kind to your dog and show her that you are trustworthy? Listen to your dog!

Remember how body language is one of our superpowers? We are always giving you information. You just need to learn how to listen to it.

Do you think this is impossible because you and your dog don't speak the same language? Well, let's explore an example that might help. Say you're petting your dog, and she gets up and walks away. This is your dog's way of saying, "Okay, that's enough for now."

Don't chase after your dog to continue petting her. Listen to what she is saying with her actions.

Or maybe you're playing fetch with your dog, and she lays down. This could mean she is tired.

Many people say: "Actions speak louder than words." This is true for your dog! And it's also true for you. What she can't say with words, she will tell you with her actions. The way you speak and respond to your dog will show her what you want.

Do you remember what I said before about the word "command"? None of us like to be commanded or spoken to in a harsh way. So, it's important to listen and respond with kindness. Speak in a gentle voice. You can quickly build trust with your dog by speaking and communicating to her in this way.

- Unconditional love is loving your dog no matter what. Your dog can have unconditional love for you too!

- Listening and following your dog's actions builds trust. You want your dog to trust you always.

- Actions speak louder than words.

CHAPTER 10

Walking Your Dog

DO YOU EVER SEE people walking with their dog, and it looks like the dog is taking the human for a walk?

That's what you DON'T want walks with your dog to look like. Also, it's important that your dog doesn't feel choked. My goal is to help your dog learn to walk next to you like a shadow.

You want your dog to be near your side. It's kind of like a fun game! When you stop, he stops. When you speed up, he speeds up.

Try one of my favorite games with your dog to practice walking! I call this the **Shadow Game**. You want your dog to follow what you do, like your shadow would follow you if you were walking outside in the sun.

So, if you take a step, your dog will take a step. And if you stop, your dog stops.

The goal of this game is to help your dog listen to you while different things are going on.

When I walk outside, there are sooo many distractions. This game helped me learn to listen even when other exciting things are happening.

Here's How to Play the Shadow Game

1. Have your dog sit next to you while you stand. Reach down and pet your dog.

2. Take one step forward. Ask your dog to take one step forward and then sit back down.

3. When your dog sits, give him a treat. This teaches him to follow you closely.

4. Then, take two steps with your dog and stop. Have your dog sit again. Tell him how great he is for doing this with you.

5. Then, give him another treat.

6. You can try different ways of doing this. Change it up! Walk in slow motion or start jogging. Walk sideways or backward. Go up and down the stairs (be careful!) or in and out of different rooms.

7. In the beginning though, go slowly. This makes it easier for your dog to learn.

Now that you know how to play, here are a few rules to keep in mind.

Rules of the game:

- Start inside your house with your dog on a leash. You can take your dog outside and try this soon but play indoors first.

- In the beginning, it may be helpful to have a few treats or pieces of kibble in your hand. Praise is my favorite treat of all. Once your dog gets the hang of things, use praise instead of treats.

- You want your puppy to follow close behind or stand right next to you. If he gets distracted or pulls to be in front of you, stop. Have your dog sit and then turn around and start walking in a different direction.

Play this game with your dog for a few days inside. Make sure your dog is listening to you and not pulling on the leash. Soon, your pup will be ready to walk outside with you!

Good leash manners are one of the most important things your dog will learn. Why? Because we need a lot of walks!

Dogs need to be walked for many reasons. Walks allow us to exercise, go potty, and catch up on the latest neighborhood gossip.

Do you enjoy catching up with your friends? So do we! We do this by sniffing and peeing in special places around the neighborhood. As dogs, we learn a lot about each other by smelling pee. It's another one of our superpowers.

Remember when we talked about scientific studies? Well, those same studies have said that sniffing also helps us to feel happy and relaxed.[1]

---

1 Duranton, C., & Horowitz, A. (2019). Let me sniff! Nosework induces positive judgment bias in pet dogs. Applied Animal Behaviour Science, 211, 61-66. https://www.sciencedirect.com/science/article/abs/pii/S0168159118304325?via%3Dihub

When my family walks me, their main job is to keep me safe. They also make sure I take care of potty business and enjoy some sniff breaks too.

You and your pup might see other dogs on your walks. This can be so fun! But there are some important things to know, too.

What to do if you see another dog on your walk:

- Only visit other dogs during your walks if you are invited.

- Be careful of other dogs, especially dogs you don't know. They might not want to say hi.

- Always ask the other person before letting your dogs meet.

- You are responsible when you walk your dog. Only do things that you are comfortable with. Do whatever you can to stay safe.

You've probably seen other people walking their dog without a leash. I love going for walks without my leash, but I had to earn this.

I learned to come every time my family calls me. They've even taught me to sit next to them any time I see a car.

While your dog is learning these skills, keep him on a leash and harness at all times.

Think of your dog's leash as a seat belt or bike helmet—it keeps your dog safe.

Let's Review

- When walking your dog, you want her to follow you everywhere, like your shadow.

- Reward your pup with treats along the way.

- Leash training is one of the most important skills your pup needs to know. It will keep you, your dog, and others safe!

- Make sure your dog is wearing a leash at all times.

CHAPTER 11

The Scoop on Picking Up Poop

HAVE YOU EVER STEPPED in dog poop? If your answer is yes, I'd like to apologize on behalf of all dogs. Yuck!

But it's not the dog's fault when you step in our poop. The person to blame is the one walking the dog. And remember what a big responsibility it is to walk your dog?

Walking your dog is about more than having fun together—even though that's awesome too!

Walking your dog also means it's your job to pick up your pup's poo. We would like to help you if we could, but we have paws! So, we need you to pick up our messes.

And if I do say so myself, dogs poop A LOT. If you have an adult dog, they might only poop once or twice a day. But puppies? They are peeing and pooping machines!

This depends on your dog's breed, though. Either way, picking up poop is a skill every kid and pup parent should know.

Picking up dog poop might feel a bit scary and even gross at first, but it's pretty simple. I have some cool tricks that make it a lot easier too.

There are a couple of different ways to pick up dog poop. This comes down to where your pup will mostly be doing her business.

Do you have a yard where your dog goes potty? Pooper scoopers are great if you're cleaning poo in your yard!

What's a pooper scooper? Well, it does just what it sounds like—it scoops poop and keeps your hands clean at the same time. Although, you should still wash your hands after. Better safe than sorry.

How to Use a Pooper Scooper

Step 1: There should be two pieces. In one hand, you will hold the piece that looks like a rake. In the other hand, hold the piece that looks like a dustpan.

Step 2: Walk around your yard and look for any stinky presents your dog has left you.

Step 3: When you find poop, use the rake to scoop the poop into the dustpan-looking piece.

Step 4: Dump all the poop you've collected into a plastic bag. This is a very important step, so make sure to remember!

Step 5: Put the poop-filled plastic bag into your outdoor trash bin. Give your pooper scooper a rinse with your outdoor hose. Then, wash your hands!

If you don't have a yard, or if your dog goes poop on a walk, you will use a poop bag instead of a pooper scooper.

The most important thing to remember is to bring poop bags every time you walk your dog.

You can get a very expensive ticket for not picking up dog poop—even as a kid! So, unless you have $500 saved up, make sure you bring poop bags on every walk.

How to Use a Poop Bag:

Step 1: Wait patiently while your dog does his business.

Step 2: Open the bag. Stick your whole hand inside the bag.

Step 3: With your hand inside the bag, grab your dog's poop. It might feel mushy or warm or hard, but you'll get used to it!

Step 4: Keep holding your dog's poo and flip your hand over, so your palm faces the sky.

Step 5: Use your free hand to turn the bag inside out. The poop should be inside the bag, and both of your hands should have stayed completely clean.

Step 6: Tie the poop bag shut and carry it until you pass a public trash can. Throw away the poop bag—and enjoy the rest of your walk!

Let's Review

- Just like humans, pups poop every day—some more than others!

- Whether you're walking your dog or playing in your yard, it's your job to pick up your dog's poop.

- Pooper scoopers are perfect for your yard, and poop bags are needed on every one of your walks.

CHAPTER 12
Meeting Other Dogs

HAVE YOU EVER FELT nervous meeting someone new? Maybe you've had a chance to meet your favorite athlete or felt shy on your first day of school.

Dogs can feel nervous meeting new people and other dogs too. It's important to keep yourself and your dog safe when you meet other dogs.

So, what should you do when you meet a new dog?

Whenever meeting a new dog, you MUST ask their owner if you can pet their dog.

When I meet someone new, my family likes to know about it. That way, they can make sure that everyone plays nice and stays safe.

Even if a dog looks friendly and happy to see you, you always have to ask for permission. If the dog's owner says you can pet their dog, you should still be careful.

Dogs like to give strangers a little sniff first. The best way to say hi to a new dog is by letting the dog come to you. Stand still where you are (keep a bit of space between you and the dog) and hold out your hand.

If the dog doesn't want to sniff your hand, then she probably doesn't want you to pet her.

If a dog doesn't want to be touched, leave her alone.

When meeting a new dog, NEVER stick your face in her face. Most of us dogs are very friendly and love cuddles. But a kid jumping in our face can be scary.

Scared dogs are the most likely to bite. So, you really don't want to scare dogs—especially those you don't know. Giving them space and time to sniff you is the best way to make a dog feel comfortable.

Now, let's talk about what to do when your dog meets a new dog.

When you introduce your dog to a new dog, it's important to follow these rules:

Rule #1: Always ask the other dog's owner if your dogs can meet.

Rule #2: Both dogs should stay on their leashes. It's best to have the leash on in case you need to pull the dogs apart.

Rule #3: Let the dogs sniff each other first. We usually like to sniff hind ends, so it's normal if your dog goes straight to the other's rear end. (This probably seems funny to you, but we dogs can learn a lot about each other from sniffing butts. It's another one of our superpowers. That's right—we're super butt-sniffers!)

Rule #4: Watch the body language of both dogs. If one dog shows signs that they're not having fun anymore, separate the dogs.

Understanding body language is really important. We dogs talk a lot with our bodies, and it helps if you understand what we're saying.

Thankfully, I know all about this!

Here are some common body language clues:

Relaxed Dog

When your dog is relaxed, he will look very soft. His eyes and ears will be in a relaxed position.

His forehead will be smooth instead of wrinkled. He might even have a small smile.

His tail will probably be level with his spine and wagging, but this looks different depending on the dog's breed. His body might also be wiggly and loose.

Scared Dog

A fearful dog will usually shrink up with her tail tucked between her legs. Her ears might be pinned back, and she may even be shaking.

Other signs of fear in dogs can be harder to spot. Some of these signals are lots of yawning, licking her lips (when there is no food nearby), or the "whale eye" (which is when you can see the whites of your dog's eyes).

These signs can be tricky to notice because they may seem normal. If you are unsure, it is best to always be careful. By speaking gently, you can help your dog stay calm.

Playful Dog

The "play bow" is an obvious sign of a happy puppy. If your dog puts her butt in the air with her front legs flat on the floor, then that's a play bow!

Your dog's tail will be wagging either level with the spine or higher if she is extra happy. She might be really bouncy too.

FYI: Dogs will sometimes snarl or growl while we're playing. This is a situation where you need to be careful. Growling can be normal play behavior. It doesn't always mean your dog is being rude.

If your dog is growling and acting playfully at the same time, you need to decide if this is aggression.

If you're unsure, ask an adult what they think. Just remember to be careful!

Dangerous Dog

It's really important to know when a dog is aggressive. Most of us dogs are nice. But a dog can be dangerous if he's protecting himself.

This dog's hackles (AKA: the hair on his back) will probably be standing up. When a dog raises his hackles, he makes himself look bigger. This is something a dog might do if he thinks he is in danger.

A dangerous dog might look really stiff. He could be looking intensely into your eyes too. His tail might be sticking straight up and even wagging a little bit.

You can sometimes tell if a dog is dangerous before he attacks.

There are some clear warnings: curled lips, showing his teeth, and a growl or snarl.

If you see a dog acting aggressively, here are some tips

- Do not turn and run away!

- Slowly back off.

- Speak in a calm, gentle voice.

- Hold your hand up in a 'stop' position.

- Don't make direct eye contact.

- Stay calm.

You need to be aware of your situation. If you're not sure whether a dog is dangerous, turn around and walk away. Then, get help from an adult.

Let's Review

- Meeting new dogs is exciting, but ask a dog's parent for permission first.

- Think like a dog when you meet them. Let them sniff your hand and watch their body language.

- It is best to introduce dogs to each other on a leash. Have an adult help you.

- If you meet a dog that seems dangerous, stay calm and find an adult to help you right away.

CHAPTER 13
Dogs in the Morning and at Night

WAKING UP TO A HAPPY DOG is the best way to start the day!

I love my family so much. I wake them up because I can't wait to spend time with them.

Many dogs like me are early risers. We are full of energy in the morning, and we need your help to begin our day.

First Steps

Some dogs live outside part time or all the time. I love to sleep outside!

If your dog lives inside the house, she probably needs to go to the bathroom in the morning.

So, that's the first part of your plan.

Then it's time for breakfast! I eat twice a day. Some dogs eat more or less.

We're usually pretty hungry in the morning.

After Breakfast Routine:

Right after eating, your dog might need to go #2. It's normal for us to do that after a meal because our bellies are small.

Understanding Your Dog's Sleeping Habits

Dogs spend most of the day sleeping. We are champion sleepers. We get about 15-16 hours of daily shuteye. Crazy, right?!

This is because we looove naps. So we don't always need a full eight hours of sleep at one time.

Here's the cool part: Dogs and humans usually sleep at the same time during the night.

Did you know that about half of us dogs in the United States sleep in the same room (or maybe even the bed) as their families?

Each family gets to decide whether their dog sleeps inside, outside, in their rooms, or in their beds.

You, as a growing kid, need at least 8 hours of sleep every night. So, make sure you're getting enough sleep if you share the bed with your dog.

Sometimes we can be bed hogs, and some dogs even snore!

Sleep is super important for your health and doing well in school and activities. Also, if you have a phone, computer, or tablet, it's a good idea to turn it off at least an hour before you go to bed.

What's a dog's favorite breakfast?

Pupcakes.

Teach Your Dog Your Morning Plan

To help your dog follow your morning routine, explain it to her. Seriously! She understands you. This is another one of her superpowers.

Before bedtime, tell your dog what you need. For example, my family tells me, "Roxy, I need to sleep until 7:00 AM tomorrow. It's important that I get enough rest tonight."

Zoomies:

When you go to school or leave the house for a while, dogs like me catch some extra Zs. By the time you're back, we're full of energy and excitement!

When you come home, it's party time for your dog. We get so excited that sometimes we get the "zoomies."

Have you ever seen a dog run super fast in circles or back and forth? That's the zoomies! It's just us expressing our energy in a funny way.

As the night comes, it's time for us to wind down. To help with that, it's good to play calmly with your dog. This could be a slow walk, a gentle brushing, or even a bedtime story. He'll learn that nighttime means it's time to relax.

Building a Routine:

Try your best to keep things the same every day. Dogs love routine! Your dog will learn when it's time to wake up, eat, and go potty in the morning. Just remember to tell her your plan.

Before going to sleep, make sure to take your dog outside for the last bathroom break of the day. Most dogs have dinner when you do, so we might go #2 one last time before bed.

Let's Review

- 🐾 Dogs love mornings. We just can't wait to spend time with you!

- 🐾 In the morning, dogs need bathroom breaks and breakfast.

- 🐾 Dogs sleep a lot—as much as 16 hours a day!

- 🐾 Play calmly with your dog at night to help her relax.

- 🐾 Before bed, take your dog for a final bathroom break.

Puppies and Grown-Up Dogs

PUPPIES ARE SUPER CUTE and playful! They are so easy to love. When people think about getting a new dog, they might imagine bringing home a tiny, fluffy puppy. Puppies are great, and families love them because they're so adorable.

But here's the thing: there are also amazing older dogs in shelters waiting for someone to adopt them.

My family got me when I was a puppy, and I've always felt loved. But not all dogs are as lucky.

Some dogs need a second chance, and that's where really special families can help.

So, if you've adopted a dog from a shelter, that's awesome! You've done something incredible and changed your dog's life.

It's important to understand what your dog's life was like before meeting you.

Did she live with a family that loved her but couldn't keep her? Or did she have a tough time where nobody cared for her?

Some dogs in shelters have been through hard times. They might be scared or need extra love to trust people again.

If your family has a rescue dog, you might need to be patient. Your pup might feel a bit nervous about joining a new family.

It's extra important to give your rescue dog space when he needs it. Dogs, just like people, want to feel safe and loved. So, make sure to show your dog that you are trustworthy.

Remember how we talked about this before? Listening to what your dog needs is the best way to earn his trust! Watch your dog's body language and only give him the attention that he wants. Always be gentle.

Introducing your dog to other pets at home, like another dog or a cat, should happen slowly. Some dogs may have never seen a cat before!

Keeping your pets separate at first can help everyone get used to each other.

Rescue dogs might already know some tricks or be potty trained. But some rescue dogs learned rules that might not work in your house.

These dogs need some extra time to learn the ropes in your family. Learning about your dog's past and being patient can help you both understand each other better.

In just a little bit, we will talk about some special **TTouches** that will help you communicate with your dog in a really amazing way.

So, whether you have a playful puppy or a grown-up rescue dog, being patient is SO important. Understanding your furry friend will help the two of you become the best of pals.

Let's Review

- A lot of families get puppies when they want a dog. Puppies need A LOT of attention.

- Rescue dogs can be puppies or older dogs.

- Some people don't know their rescue dog's past. Be extra patient and gentle with a rescue dog.

- Talk to your family about whether a puppy or a rescue dog is the right fit for you.

CHAPTER 15
How to Show Your Dog Love with TTouches

THE TELLINGTON TTOUCH is an excellent way to show your dog love. **TTouches**® were created by a wonderful woman named Linda Tellington-Jones.

She has been working with animals for over 60 years. And not just dogs! She has worked with tigers, elephants, horses, and bunnies, just to name a few. Many veterinarians use these magic **TTouches** to help calm or help animals that are sick.

Here is how to do these easy TTouches

Imagine tiny old-fashioned clocks on your dog's body. With the tips of your fingers, draw a circle going toward the right. You want to circle around like the arrow on the clock one full time plus another one-quarter of the way.

Do you know how to read one of these clocks? You will start at 9, circle all the way around back to 9 and then a bit more to finish on the 12. See? Simple!

When my family gives me **TTouches**, I feel calm and happy. I love going to horse practice with them because **TTouches** were actually invented for horses. My family uses them on the horses they ride.

TTouches are like special circles you draw on your dog's skin with your fingers. These gentle circles help your dog relax and feel happy.

When I feel sick or scared, **TTouches** help me feel stronger and braver. They also make me feel better if I'm not feeling well.

Most importantly, they make me feel calm.

Because you want your dog to feel calm too, try some gentle **TTouches**. They should help your dog feel relaxed, so think of relaxing thoughts while you do **TTouches** on your dog.

Sometimes, my family uses the very tips of their fingers to make extra soft circles. Other times, they will use the top half of their fingers to make the circles more like a gentle massage.

How do these tiny circles help your dog feel better? Think of your favorite superhero. They need a message to know when there's trouble. TTouches signal your dog's superpowers to help him relax and feel better. If you think calm, happy thoughts while doing **TTouches**, you send calm, happy messages to her whole body.

TTouches are fantastic when your dog is scared, stressed, or trying something new.

They can even help with carsickness, especially if you do them on your dog's ears.

If your dog doesn't like car rides, try giving her some **TTouches**. It might help her feel better.

And who knows, she might even learn to love car rides!

You can learn more about **TTouches** here.

What do you call a wild dog that meditates?

Aware wolf.

Let's Review

🐾 TTouches are a wonderful way to help your dog feel better immediately.

🐾 Use these circular touches gently to help your dog feel calm.

🐾 You can also use TTouches instead of treats to reward your dog for listening so well.

CHAPTER 16

How I Learned Potty Training

LET'S TALK ABOUT AN important topic: How to teach your dog where to potty!

When you're helping your pup learn where to go potty, it's important to think like a dog.

We don't know where it's okay to go until you show us. Accidents can happen. We're animals, and we're still learning.

If your dog has an accident, please don't yell. Instead, show your dog what to do next time.

You can guide your dog by taking him to the same place every time he goes potty. Make sure everyone in your family knows to go to the same place.

When your dog goes potty in the right spot, celebrate! Pet him, give him some **TTouches**, and maybe give him a treat. This helps your dog understand where to go potty.

Now that I am potty trained, I tell my family when I have to go.

Some dogs bark at the door, others use bells, and some have other ways to let you know it's time. Talk to your family about what will work best in your home.

Now, about keeping your house clean, especially if you have a puppy: Let's think about how humans and dogs are different.

Human babies wear diapers, right? Well, that's because they can't use the toilet. Puppies won't wear diapers, so we use crates. Crates keep us in one spot, which helps us from making a big mess inside the house.

Most puppies or dogs find that the crate is a cozy spot. When we're inside, we have fewer accidents around the house. This is how my family potty trained me. I'm so glad I learned how to love my crate!

For most dogs, crate training is temporary. Some dogs learn to love their crate so much that they even want to have it after they are potty trained! Other dogs may want to sleep in their crate at night.

You might feel sad to keep your dog in a crate, but it helps with learning.

You can make it comfy with towels, blankets, and a shirt that smells like you. Give your dog toys to enjoy inside the crate too. This is especially important if you bring home a new puppy.

You may want to bring something from where the puppy lived before, like a blanket he may have slept on, to help him feel safe. This reminds your puppy of his mother or brothers and sisters.

And some dogs love our crates. We like to curl up in cozy places to relax. So, make your dog's crate really nice!

Sometimes, I go to my crate when I want some alone time. Your dog may do the same thing.

Respect that your dog might want some space, just like humans need alone time too. After recharging, your dog will be ready to hang out with you again!

Let's Review

- Celebrate when your dog goes potty in the right spot.
- Crates are cozy spots that help with potty training.
- Help your dog feel comfortable in her crate by using toys and TTouches.
- Respect your dog's alone time!
- My family wrote a whole book on potty training if you'd like to learn more.

CHAPTER 17

Happy Hellos and Jumping Pups

HAS YOUR DOG EVER jumped up to say hello? It might feel nice for you. But not everyone likes it, especially if they don't know your dog.

Whether a dog is big or small, jumping can be painful or even scary.

Think about all the manners you've learned. You've probably been taught to say things like "Please," "Thank you," and "Excuse me."

Teaching your dog not to jump up is like teaching him manners. People will be glad to meet your dog if he isn't jumping on them.

Your dog's paws might be dirty, muddy or who knows what! Dirty paws can ruin clothes, so it's best to teach your dog polite greetings.

Do you want to know why dogs jump up on you? Well, it's because we're just so excited to see you. We want to hug you and kiss your face.

But just because we like it doesn't mean we should do it. You don't want your dog knocking over grandma when she comes to visit!

Your dog won't know that he could knock someone over, so you need to teach him. The best way to teach your dog is by asking him to sit every time he is called.

Remember the 3 most important things to teach your dog?

Sit, stay, and come!

Let's practice

Ask your dog to sit and stay. Then call him to come over. Remember to be polite. When he comes, he should sit in front of you or next to you. Reward him with TTouches and kind words. This helps him learn to sit when greeting.

You should also teach your dog to stop and sit before he goes out the door or gets into a car. You just want your dog to sit every time you ask!

If your dog jumps on you, don't reward him by telling him he's a good boy or loving on him for jumping up.

I know that we all get excited and want to be close together. It's tough to tell your dog not to jump on you. But it's the best way.

Teaching your dog not to jump up is like teaching him manners. People will be glad to meet your dog if he isn't jumping on them.

Your dog's paws might be dirty, muddy or who knows what! Dirty paws can ruin clothes, so it's best to teach your dog polite greetings.

Do you want to know why dogs jump up on you? Well, it's because we're just so excited to see you. We want to hug you and kiss your face.

But just because we like it doesn't mean we should do it. You don't want your dog knocking over grandma when she comes to visit!

Your dog won't know that he could knock someone over, so you need to teach him. The best way to teach your dog is by asking him to sit every time he is called.

Remember the 3 most important things to teach your dog?

Sit, stay, and come!

Let's practice

Ask your dog to sit and stay. Then call him to come over. Remember to be polite. When he comes, he should sit in front of you or next to you. Reward him with TTouches and kind words. This helps him learn to sit when greeting.

Good girl, Roxy. Thank you for waiting before we go outside.

You should also teach your dog to stop and sit before he goes out the door or gets into a car. You just want your dog to sit every time you ask!

If your dog jumps on you, don't reward him by telling him he's a good boy or loving on him for jumping up.

I know that we all get excited and want to be close together. It's tough to tell your dog not to jump on you. But it's the best way.

If you get excited when your dog jumps, he will think jumping is good. Ask your puppy to sit, then give him praise and **TTouches**.

What did the dog say after he jumped on his owner and got her muddy?

"Please fur-give me."

Let's Review

- Dogs jump when we're excited, but this can cause problems.

- Teach your dog to sit when called for a polite greeting.

- Practice sit, stay, and come to help your dog learn good manners.

- Give your dog treats and TTouches when he sits for a happy hello!

CHAPTER 18

Your Family is Not a Wolf Pack

REMEMBER HOW WE SAID before that dogs' ancestors are wolves?

But guess what? Things have changed a lot since then! Now, dogs and humans have a special bond. We do all sorts of things together.

We can make you happy when you're sad, use our super sniffing powers, run and play together and we can even help keep you safe. We're more than friends. We're family.

Think about your family for a moment. Imagine your parents, siblings, maybe grandparents or others.

When you imagine your family, do you picture your dog? That's because we're an important part of many families' lives!

My life is all about sleeping with the AC on, swimming in the ocean, going for car rides, and cuddling with my humans. Wolves don't do any of that!

Some dogs even share the bed with their family. Would you invite a wolf to share your bed? Probably not! Haven't you heard about the Big Bad Wolf?

Every family is unique and special. And dogs can make a family even more special!

    Some people and some dog trainers see dogs as "friendly wolves." Some dog trainers say your dog thinks they are part of a wolf pack.

    We're not wolves, though. Not even close!

    Some people want to think dogs and wolves are the same, but we are dogs!

    And we dogs recognize that we live with humans and are not wolves. So, there is no reason to treat us like members of a wolf pack.

Some trainers say that you need to be the Alpha wolf to train a dog and they do that by punishing, choking, or shocking a dog.

Please don't "alpha" your dog. There is no need to choke, hit, or yell at her. This will make your dog feel very sad. And you may miss one of the more important relationships in your life.

Instead, welcome your dog as part of the family!

Wolves live in packs, but your dog isn't part of a wolf pack. She's part of YOUR family. So, treat her like family. Be patient, forgive her mistakes, and encourage her when she's scared. Remember, we dogs love you fur-ever!

Let's Review

- 🐾 Dogs like me came from wolves, but we're family dogs now. There is no need to treat us like wolves.

- 🐾 Treat your dog with kindness and respect, just like you do with your human family.

- 🐾 Your dog is part of your family and will love you unconditionally!

CHAPTER 19

Woof!

WOULDN'T IT BE COOL if dogs could talk to you in words you understood? Maybe in the future, there'll be technology for that. Who knows?

But for now, we'll keep talking to you in our special way.

Have you ever noticed that our "woofs" sound different? That's because we have different barks for different moods.

My barks sound different than my friend Joey, who is a Toy Poodle. I have big barks, and he has small barks. Like humans have different voices, your dog has a unique bark "voice." What do your dog's barks sound like?

"Play with me!"

When I was a puppy, I wanted to play all the time. I'd bark like, "Hey! Play with me!"

But guess what? Barking didn't work. My family was smart. They played with me when I stopped barking.

So, be patient with your dog's request for fun until he's quiet. When he sits and waits like I showed you, then give him love and attention. This teaches him not to bark so much.

"I'm bored!"

Dogs sometimes bark when they're bored. It usually sounds really repetitive. If your dog does this, wait for her to stop barking.

Once she's quiet, play with her or take her for a walk. This will be so exciting that she'll forget all about barking!

If your dog is outside barking at nothing, call her inside. She might just be missing you! See if she stops barking when she's with you.

This is also a perfect time for a 1 minute training session. Practice a few rounds of sit, stay, and come and see if the barking stops.

"Something is wrong!"

This bark is intense. If I think something's wrong, I bark a lot. I also make sure to be very loud, so everyone knows I'm worried.

My family is usually thankful that I am looking out for them.

Your dog wants to keep you safe, even if it's just a friend coming over.

"I'm so excited!"

Some dogs bark because they're really excited. This happens to me sometimes when I am playing outside with my family. Life is just too good!

But I needed to learn how to be quiet when asked.

If you don't want your dog to bark when you play, here's what I recommend:

End the game when your dog barks.

Then practice: sit, stay and come. Once your dog stops barking, you can keep playing your game. Your dog will quickly learn to play quietly.

"Ouch!"

Dogs yelp when they're in pain or sad. If your dog yelps randomly, check if she's okay. Get some help from an adult if your dog is hurt.

If your dog is barking, stay calm. If you yell at your dog for barking, he will just think you are barking back. Then you'll be in a bark-off!

Instead of yelling, think about what makes your dog confident. Do a 1 minute training session.

Once your dog is focused, say, "I need you to stop barking, please." He should quiet down. Then, give him treats and love for being good.

Let's Review

🐾 Dogs have unique barks to talk to you.

🐾 Learn what your dog's barks mean. This may take some time since each dog's barks are special. If you pay attention, you will learn.

🐾 Stay calm to help your dog calm down.

🐾 Please don't yell at your dog for barking. This can only make the barking worse!

CHAPTER 20

Bath Time Fun

HAVE YOU EVER BEEN splashed or pushed into freezing cold water? It can be a real shock! And it isn't very fun, especially if you were hoping to stay dry.

Well, that's how your dog might feel about bath time. But I will show you how to make it fun for everyone!

You want your dog to love baths. Let me share how I like baths, and you can try the same with your dog.

Remember to ask a grown-up for help. Some dogs get really hyper during baths. Getting all wet makes us so silly!

When my family gave me my first bath, they started slowly. We hung out in the bathtub without water, and they even fed me treats for being calm.

Baths make me happy because I learned that being in the tub means I get treats. The next day, my family took me to the tub again, and I got more treats for being good—yay!

Then, they turned on the water, but they didn't spray me with it yet. They only turned it on, so I knew what to expect. I got even more treats!

I taste-tested the water, so your dog might want to do this too. Make sure the water is warm, so you don't frighten your dog with ice-cold water. Check that the water isn't hot either. We have sensitive skin, so hot water can hurt!

If your dog seems a little afraid of the bath, have an adult help you and practice **TTouches** before or during the bath. It also helps to talk to your dog in a soothing voice.

Finally, it was time to start the bath. My family filled a bowl with warm water and slowly poured it over my back first. I was really glad they didn't spray me in the face with water—I definitely would NOT have liked that.

Some people give their dogs a bath outside. That's okay, but it helps if the water can be warm.

My family used the bowl to gently pour water all over me. I was soaking wet, which made me want to shake off all the water. I gave my very best shake, and water went EVERYWHERE.

Everyone laughed, and before we knew it, we were all soaking wet. That's kind of how every bath goes, and it's also why it's so fun!

They were very careful not to get soap in my eyes or water in my ears. Then, they rinsed off all the soap. I was kind enough to rinse everyone else too.

After a few more big shakes, my first bath was done. I would say it went pretty well.

Once I got out of the tub, I was super hyper—I had the zoomies! Something about being all wet just makes me go crazy!

I'm really silly and playful after a bath, and sometimes I want to roll around in the grass or dirt. My family isn't always very excited about that.

What can I say? Just soak up the good-smelling cuddles while you can get them!

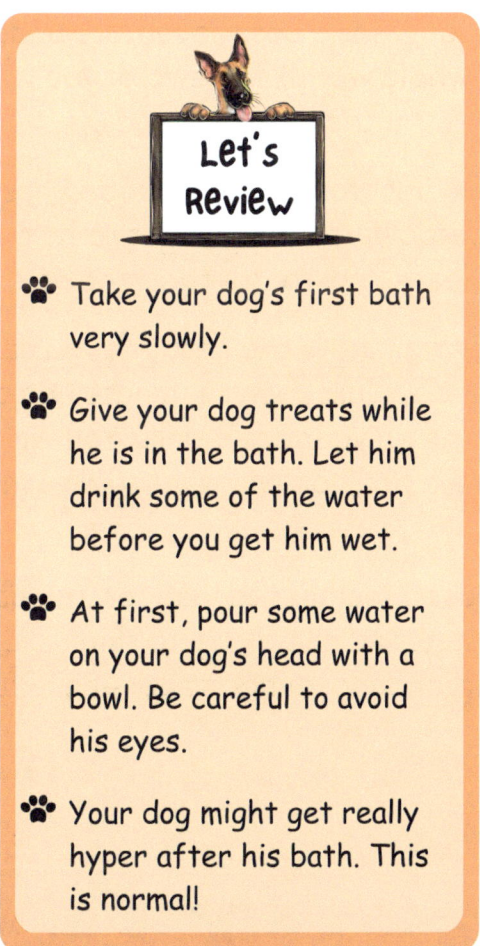

Let's Review

- Take your dog's first bath very slowly.

- Give your dog treats while he is in the bath. Let him drink some of the water before you get him wet.

- At first, pour some water on your dog's head with a bowl. Be careful to avoid his eyes.

- Your dog might get really hyper after his bath. This is normal!

Thank you so much for reading my book!

I want to wish you good luck. You have a very fun adventure ahead of you. And your dog is the best adventure buddy in the whole world! The two of you will be the best of friends.

Just remember, your dog has superpowers! And you get to help him learn how to use those powers.

Dog training is the best gift you can give your dog. Just spend 1 minute at a time working on your dog's skills. You will have so much fun, you will want to do 1 minute sessions all day long!

Just remember to work on the basics (sit, stay, and come), try to think like your dog, and most importantly–have fun!!

Can I Ask For a Small Favor?

I love feedback! Please share what you liked or hoped to learn more about. I truly value your thoughts.

I would be incredibly grateful if you took the time to review this book on Amazon by scanning the QR code below. Thank you!

I also want to give you a free gift.

You like gifts, right? Please visit **1minutedog.com** and you can have a FREE dog training video course. I am in some of the videos. Yahoo!

SCAN ME

to Watch the FREE Videos
& Get the Guides

Do you want to see me and some of my friends in action? You can on the **1minutedog.com** website!

There are also other books and lots of blogs. One of my favorite blogs teaches you how to have a dog's birthday party! Visit **1minutedog.com** to read more.

For all things dog training, check out the 1 Minute Dog website, **1minutedog.com.** Please sign up for special discounts and other books I am working on. I have a lot more to share!

Unfortunately, I cannot answer individual dog training questions unless you are a client. You can check in with me, though, if you'd like. If you are over 13, you may send an email to info@1minutedog.com. If you are under 13, ask your parents to reach out to me!

You can explore a wide variety of instructional training videos, helpful tips on the blog, more information on my background, and of course, lots of cute dog photos!

These are some of my favorite dog friends from over the years!

And here is my best friend, Roxy!

Thanks for spending time with us.

Made in the USA
Thornton, CO
07/28/24 02:09:44

e6e16e61-a1b6-4494-b607-07a7e3a177c2R01